Scary Faces

And Other Arty Face Paintings

Scary Faces

And Other Arty Face Paintings

CARO CHILDS

p

This is a Parragon Publishing Book
This edition published 2002

Parragon Publishing
Queen Street House
4 Queen Street
Bath BA1 1HE, UK

Designed, produced and packaged by Stonecastle Graphics Ltd

Design by Paul Turner and Sue Pressley
Photography by Roddy Paine
Face painting by Caro Childs
Edited by Gillian Haslam and Philip de Ste. Croix

ISBN 0-75258-691-2

Printed in China

With thanks to our models:
Asher Edge Blake, Sam Little, Emily Lumb, Sam Lumb, Matthew Oakley, Becky Paine, Josie Paine, Nat Paine, Tashi Petter, Nicholas St. Clair, Letitia Thomas, and Reece Woodhams.

Thanks to Sophie Reissner for the Warthog design and Bibi Freeman for the Space Monster.

Disclaimer:
Face painting should be fun and safe. Always check that your model does not suffer from any allergies. Do not paint children under two years old, or anyone who has a facial cut, sore skin, or sore eyes. Always use proprietary face paints specifically designed for this use and follow all safety instructions. The publisher and their agents cannot accept liability for any loss, damage, or injury however caused.

Contents

Introduction

Have you ever wondered what it would be like to be someone else or even how it would feel to be an animal? Well, with the help of this book, you could begin to find out.

Face painting is a bit like wearing a mask but, because your face moves, it is more realistic, so more fun and more exciting. Face painting is great fun to do and even adults really want to have a go, so you will probably get lots of help. You can make-up yourself but it is easier to paint a friend.

This is what you will need to start face painting:

• A set of professional water-based make-up. You can use powder blushers, lipsticks, glitter gels, and metallic face paints as well if you wish.

• Two or three paintbrushes. It is useful to have a fine pointed one and a larger thick one. A straight cut brush is very good because it can be used to make a thick or thin mark. It is important to use brushes that are nice and soft on the skin. Sable is the best material but synthetic watercolor brushes or make-up brushes are good too.

• Some make-up sponges. You can buy sponges, brushes, and face paint from fancy dress shops and theater shops.

Safety Code

• Keep your make-up very clean and always wash your sponges and brushes, after using them, in warm soapy water, then rinse and dry them thoroughly. They will last much longer if you look after them. Professional water-based make-up has special anti-fungicides in it so it is not necessary to use any sort of disinfectant, just clean water.

• Don't paint children under two years old.

• Don't paint anyone who has a facial cut or sore skin.

• Don't paint anyone who has sore eyes.

• Always ask your model if they suffer from any allergies to food or soaps and, if so, it is better not to paint them.

You will also need:

- A pot of clean water.
- A towel or flannel on which to keep your sponges.
- A mirror to show your model what you have created.
- A comfortable place to work. A folding table and two folding chairs are ideal but, of course, you can work at your dining table. Just make sure that you cover it up well, in case of spills.

Always work in good light so that you can see the colors. Spread a towel on your table and set out your paints, water, and brushes. Place two chairs facing each other on one side of the table and sit so that the light falls on your model's face. It is important to sit close with your model's knees between yours so that their body is not twisted to one side. Place your free hand on your model's head; just use your fingertips. That way you can turn your model from side to side while you are painting and he or she will not twitch so much if your hand is on their head.

Remember to talk to your model so they are not nervous and be gentle as it may be your turn next!

When you have finished, remember to take some photographs before your design is washed off. Keep your photographs in a scrapbook and add pictures from cartoons and films or photographs of real animals. These will help you to build up a portfolio of good ideas.

Once you have got the knack of face painting, you will find that everyone wants your help at school plays, fêtes, fundraising events, and parties. If you are going to paint other people, it is important to follow a safety code so that you never cause anyone, including yourself, a health problem.

Did You Know?

That Ancient British warriors painted themselves blue to frighten their enemies. They used a blue dye called woad that is made from a yellow flower!

But the earliest known make-up artists were the ancient Egyptians who lived in the first dynasty 5000 years ago. There is a beautiful Egyptian make-up box in the British Museum in London.

Scary Scarecrow

A friendly scarecrow watching over a farmer's crops is a traditional sight when you are in the country. Sometimes a scarecrow looks *too* friendly and you may see a couple of crows sitting on his arms who are not scared at all. In some parts of France the villagers often make life-size stuffed rag dolls which look very much like scarecrows, and it is quite a common sight to find one sitting on a bench in the center of a French village!

Arty Tip:

Try mixing colors together.
Red and Yellow = Orange
Yellow and Blue = Green
Red and Blue = Purple
Red and Green = Brown

You can make colors lighter and darker by adding white or black.

Of course your model's skin color will change the paint shade a bit, so you may need to experiment.

A scarecrow make-up is simple, so it is a good design with which to learn the basic skills of face painting. It is also very good for a fancy dress party as the costume is easy to put together.

1 Dip a sponge into the water and squeeze it out very well, then rub it in some light brown paint.

2 Holding the model's head firmly with your free hand, press the sponge on to their face. Try to move the sponge in small circles rather than long wipes to avoid making streaks. Ask your model to close their eyes and be careful as you sponge over the eyelids.

You want to achieve an even base, but scarecrows don't mind being a bit messy.

If the paint is streaky, your sponge is too wet. If the paint won't go on at all, it is too dry. You may find it easier to wet the paint rather than the sponge when you want to add more paint.

You will need:

To paint this scarecrow you will need light brown, red, yellow, and black face paint. Set up your paints and sit comfortably opposite your model.

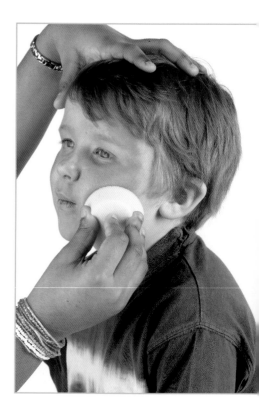

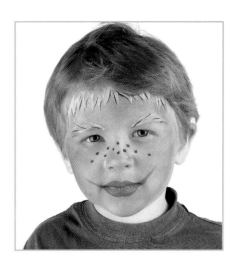

4 Add a straw fringe by mixing some water into the yellow paint. Using a paintbrush, paint yellow lines from the top of the forehead to the eyebrows. Paint over the eyebrows with yellow lines that look like straw. With a clean brush mix up some red paint and paint a smiley mouth.

5 Finish the scarecrow by painting some black lines next to the yellow lines to look like shadows; then paint a few dots to give the scarecrow some freckles. Use the very tip of your paintbrush.

3 Use the other side of your sponge or a clean one to apply some red paint to the cheeks.

Arty Tip:

When you are using a paintbrush the make-up should be quite wet. Mix up a puddle of paint that you can dip into. The paint should flow off the brush in a smooth line but not drip once it is on the skin.

Loyal Sheepdog

The sheepdog is one of the most useful animals on a farm and definitely man's best friend, but those herding skills were learned long ago when the sheepdog's ancestors were wolves hunting in packs.

You will need:

Black, brown, white, and red paint and some hairbands.

See if you can make your model look like a sheepdog, or if you have a favorite dog, adapt these instructions to your own design.
It helps to have a photograph of the dog as a reference.

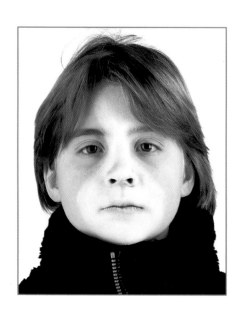

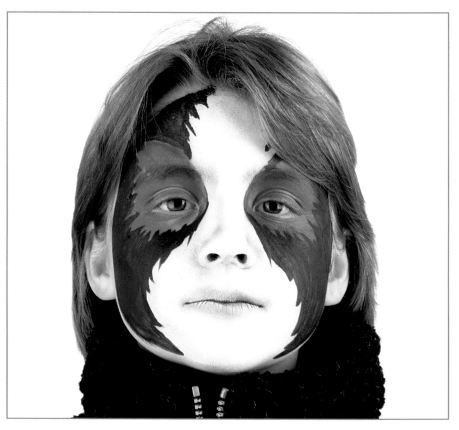

1 Sponge a white stripe down the center of your model's face and widen it out at the bottom of the face to cover the area under the nose, including the mouth and chin.

2 Sponge brown paint over the eyelids, then load a brush with black and paint around the sides of the face. Use the paintbrush to paint a shaggy edge where the black make-up meets the brown and white make-up. Remember to make the painted edges imitate the lines of a dog's fur.

3 Paint a mouth shape in black. Try to make it slant upward to give the dog a pointed face. Paint a pink nose, a red lolloping tongue, and white canine teeth. Outline the tongue with black paint and fill in the mouth shape also with black.

You can tie your model's hair into bunches to resemble ears.

4 Paint a black line from under the nose to the mouth and paint a small line down the middle of the tongue. Now you have created a very realistic-looking sheepdog.

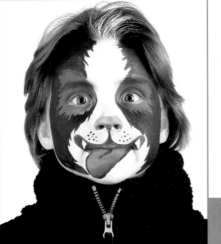

Arty Tip:

Let the make-up dry for a few seconds before you paint an outline around details. Draw in the shapes of the teeth with a thin black line before filling them in with white.

Porky Pig

People often ask to be painted as a pig, perhaps because they like the idea of being sweet sugar pink. Or maybe recent pig movie stars have made the role of porker more attractive! Whatever their reasons, it is a fun face to paint, but don't be fooled into thinking that a simple color scheme means a simple face. You will have to be very careful with the outline to make sure your model changes into a realistic pig.

You will need:

You will need three shades of pink paint. Mix plenty of pink before you start, using red and white. Add more red to make a darker pink for painting details. Add white to make a pale pink for the base.

1 Sponge a pale pink base all over your model's face.

2 Load a broad paintbrush with pink paint. Outline the shape of the top of a pig's head, its ears, cheeks, and chin, as in the picture. Fill in the whole area with pale pink. Add some red paint to your sponge and make rosy cheeks and blushing ears.

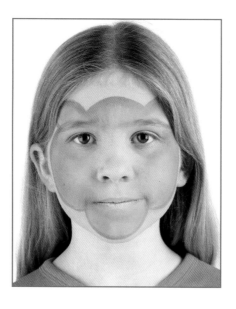

Arty Tip:

Before the paint has dried, take a slightly damp sponge and pull the paint in toward the middle of the face all the way around the outline so that you do not get a hard line on the inside edge of the outline. This is called drag blending.

3 Using a darker pink and a fine paintbrush, make a circle from just below the middle of your model's nose to just above the lip. It should extend out onto the model's cheeks.

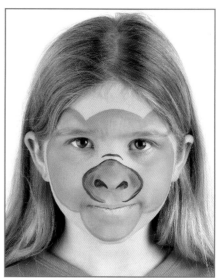

4 Using black paint and a fine pointed brush, make black nostril holes on either side of your model's nose (above the real nostrils) and outline the shape of the nose.

5 Using the same fine brush, carefully outline the ear. Look at the picture to see which way the lines must go.

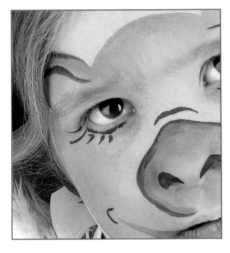

6 With black paint and a clean brush, paint a line underneath the lower lid. If your pig is a girl, she might like false eyelashes painted on her cheeks.

7 Finally paint your model's lower lip dark pink and extend the smile onto the cheeks. Add some fine lines and dimples around the mouth.

Arty Tip:

When painting on, or near, your model's eyes be very careful and gentle. When you paint a line under the eye, ask your model to look up at the ceiling but without lifting up their chin. This makes painting much easier. Remember to be reassuring; professional face paint will not do any harm even if it does get into the eyes. If your model is young or fidgety, it is better not to paint the lines too close to the eyelashes.

Strutting Cockerel

Welcoming the dawn with his loud "cock a doodle doo," the farmyard cockerel makes sure everyone is up early. He is quite sure who rules the roost on his farm as he proudly struts around the farmyard showing off to the chickens.

You will need:
Yellow, red, blue, green, and black face paint to recreate the rooster make-up shown here.

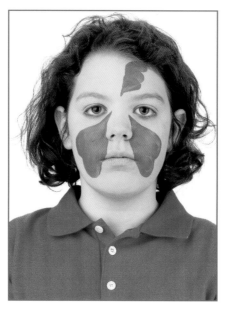

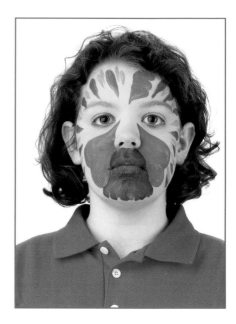

1 First of all, sponge a warm yellow color evenly over the sides, middle, and forehead of your model's face.

2 Next take a broad brush and mix up some red paint. Paint a line down the center of your model's forehead, stopping between the eyebrows above the top of the nose. Paint a big loop and three smaller loops to one side of this line. Fill in any gaps.

3 Load the same brush with more red paint and, starting at a point below the eye on the side of the nose, sweep the brush diagonally down across the cheek. Curl the line round with two loops and take it back up the side of the nose to the start point. It should look like an upside-down heart. Make the same shape on the other side of the face. Fill them both in with red paint.

4 Use a clean brush and blue paint to fill in the area under your model's nose down to the chin. Paint over your model's lips. Paint plenty of blue feathers around your model's face. Wash your brush and paint in some green feathers too.

Arty Tip:
If you want to make your model's nose look more pointy, paint the sides of the nose blue too.

Oranges and Lemons

Yellow make-up comes in different shades. It can be a cool citrus color with a hint of green or a warm eggy yellow that is almost orange.

You can add red to a cool yellow to make it warmer but you cannot make a warm yellow more lemony. If you only have one yellow, make sure it is a bright lemon yellow, but you may want to buy all the shades.

5 To finish your rooster, use a fine pointed brush and black paint. Outline the cockerel's comb and wattles. Paint a line from the top of the wattles over the eyebrows and around the eyes. Paint two little lines on the nose to make nostrils in the rooster's beak.

6 Outline some of the feathers on the chin and also around the eyes and forehead.

Glittery Peacock

Mardi Gras is traditionally a time for feasting and carnivals before the season of fasting. Caribbean carnivals held at this time are famous for their amazing costumes and headdresses; beautiful glittery dancers share the stage with more sinister figures. In Venice the emphasis is on masks, both grotesque and elegant. This make-up will help you to recreate a carnival atmosphere. Nothing is more famous for its looks than a shimmering peacock such as this.

You will need:

To become this glamorous creature use turquoise, gold, copper, yellow, blue, green, white, and black make-up. You can use glitter in any color or even multi-color if you have some.

Arty Tip:

You can buy water-based pearlized and metallic make-up in many shades.

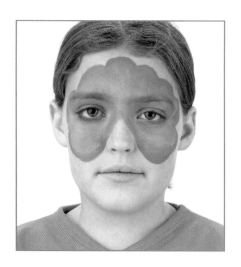

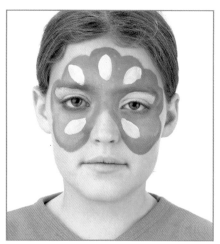

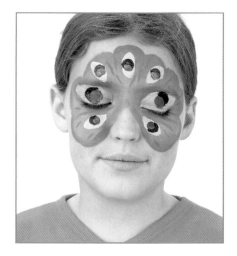

1 Mix up a turquoise color using blue and green and white make-up if you have not got turquoise. Paint an open fan-shaped outline of a peacock's tail around the edge of the model's face. While it is still damp, pull the color toward the center using a sponge.

2 Ask your model to close their eyes and, using a clean brush, paint the eyelids yellow. Paint five more yellow eye shapes around the peacock's tail. Position them so they point toward the bridge of your model's nose.

3 Paint a blue round shape in the center of each yellow "eye." Paint a black crescent on the outer edge of the blue center.

Safety Tip:

Only use glitter that is sold as make-up. Any other sort may scratch the skin. Be careful not to let any glitter get into the model's eyes.

Glitter gel is best applied when the make-up has dried. Loose powder glitter is very fine and can be dusted on to wet make-up but it does tend to get everywhere!

4 Paint a copper peacock in the center of your model's nose. Paint gold and white lines radiating out from the peacock. Paint gold crescents on the blue centers of the "eye" shapes.

5 Finish by painting a curly dark blue line around the outside of your design and around your model's eyes. Add glitter and blue lips for a glamorous carnival look.

Hummingbirds

Hummingbirds are beautiful delicate creatures that hover like tiny jewels to sip nectar from tropical flowers. They beat their wings so fast that they really do make a humming noise. This design is also about fantasy birds full of glitter and sparkle. It is a fabulous carnival face that you can paint in any color.

One of the reasons that this face is very popular, especially with dancers and party-goers, is that it does not use an all-over base so you can eat and drink without fear of damaging your make-up.

1 Choose colors that look good with your model's clothes. If you like pastel colors, be sure to include at least one strong color that will show up as well.

2 Ask your model to close her eyes and, with a medium brush and your main color, paint over the eyelid and eyebrow in an oval shape to make a bird's body.

3 Paint in a bird's head and beak. Paint a beautiful curling tail and make two oval loops at the end of the tail feathers.

4 Use a clean brush to paint stripes of colored wings at two points over the eyebrow. Paint the same colors into the tail loops.

5 Paint an exotic flower over and around the other eye. Use your imagination to be as decorative and glamorous with your painting as you want. Outline your design to make sure it will stand out in a crowd and then just "Party On."

You will need:

Three or four colors that go together and match your model's outfit. You choose!

Some people might think that this face is just *too* bright, but if you can wear bold pinks, turquoise, and glitter, go for it!

Arty Tip:

Whenever you paint a face, it is important to pay attention to the colors your model is wearing or maybe to their skin coloring or the colors of their eyes. This doesn't mean you have to match colors exactly, regardless of the design you are painting, but it does mean that where a choice is possible, you need to make a decision. For example, when you paint a dog's tongue, should you choose a bright pink or a rusty red? Either could work, but the one which will make your design look really great depends on your model. Experiment and remember to take photographs, as this will help you to improve.

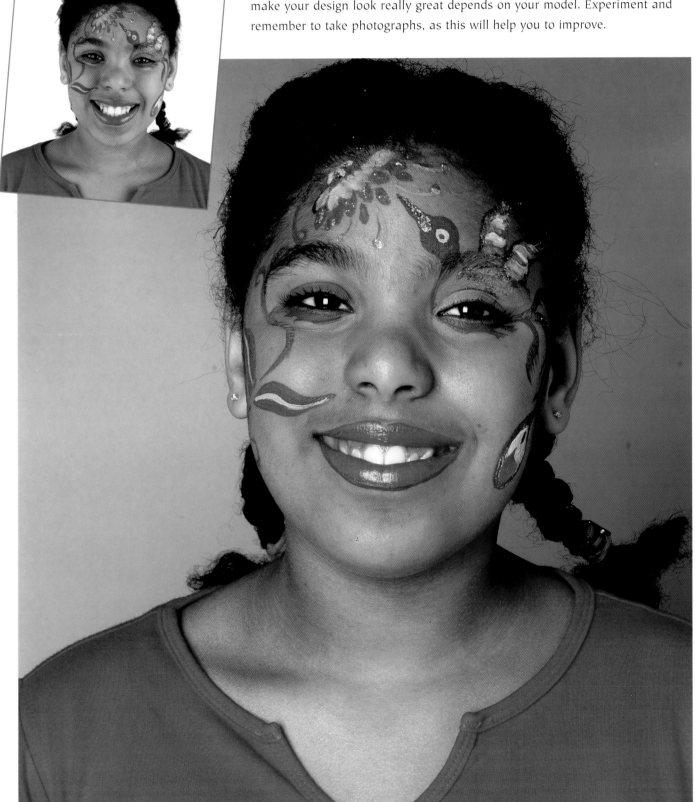

Harlequin Jester

The Harlequin or Joker is an elusive figure. Always laughing, he is fun to be with, but you can never be sure if he is laughing at you or with you. He is a two-faced creature who mocks everything. If you decide to be the Harlequin, watch out as the joke may turn out to be on you.

You will need:
Black, white, and red make-up.

Joker's Riddle
What is black and white and "red" all over?
A newspaper.

This Harlequin is rather like the joker in a deck of cards.

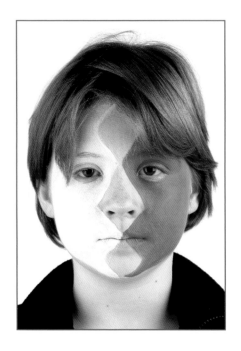

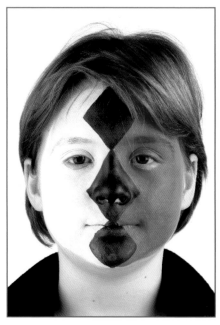

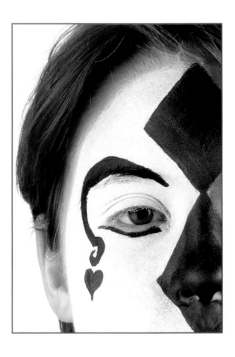

1 Start by outlining the diamond shapes down the center of the face using white paint. Sponge white paint away from this line all over one side of the model's face. Try to make a smooth base so that no skin shows through. Do the same thing with red paint on the other side of the face.

2 Fill in the diamond shapes with black paint. This face depends on clean strong lines and although it is a simple design, you have to be careful to let the make-up dry before moving on to the next stage.

3 Use a fine paintbrush to underline the eyes and paint contrasting eyebrows with black paint. Use your imagination to make eyebrows that suit the Harlequin's personality. One of these droops down and ends in a point with a little heart, but they could end with an arrowhead or curl upward.

4 Finish this tricky two-faced character by painting a laughing mouth. Paint red lips on the white side of the face and white lips on the other side.

Arty Tip:

If you find it hard to draw diamonds with symmetrical sides, try this tip. Take a 2in x 2in (5cm x 5cm) square of paper. Fold it in half along the diagonal. Fold it in half again across the longest side and, with a pair of scissors, cut along the open edge from half way along the fold to the opposite point. Open out the paper and you should have a perfect diamond. You can use it as a stencil by holding it in place on your model and sponging over the edge of it. When you take it away, a diamond shape will be revealed.

Red Devil Mask

The two designs shown on these pages are typical of the kind of masks worn in Venice at carnival time. They would also be great to wear for a Halloween party. Face paint applied like a mask, covering only the top half of the face, is very comfortable to wear at a party because you are able to eat and drink without spoiling your make-up.

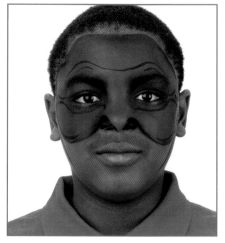

When painting a mask, it is important not to go right to the outside of the face. In both of these designs, a painted false ribbon dangles down the side of the face from the edge of the mask, giving a *trompe l'oeil* effect.

1 Paint the outline of the devil mask with red paint. Some people think it is easier to paint the left side first if you are right-handed, and vice versa. However, if you turn your model's head so that one side of the face is directly in front of you, it should be easy to do whichever side you tackle first.

2 Make sure the outline is symmetrical before you start filling it in.

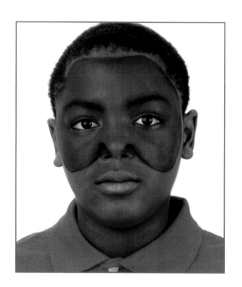

3 Use a sponge to fill in the shape of the mask but be careful not to spoil the outline.

You will need:

Some gold glitter or gold crème make-up for the devil's horns, as well as red and black paint.

4 Shade the eye sockets with black and add wrinkle lines in dark red. Give the devil smile lines as he is at a carnival!

5 Paint gold horns above the eyebrows. Paint in black twisting ribbons. Use a straight cut brush and keep your hand at the same angle while painting twists. They should come out thick and thin just as when using an italic nib pen. Add some glitter and gold highlights.

Witch's Cat

The instructions are for the Red Devil Mask but by looking at the picture below, you will be able to adapt it for the Witch's Cat. The important part is to get the outline right. Use black for the outline but drag blend it with red to create this cat mask.

Frankenstein

Poor Frankenstein's monster was made from scraps and pieces of other people's dead bodies, and then brought back to life. He is truly scary, but he only wants to be friendly. We tend to call him Frankenstein but really that was the name of the mad scientist who created him. The book in which he first appeared is a classic horror tale written in 1818 by Mary Shelley.

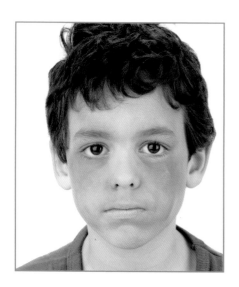

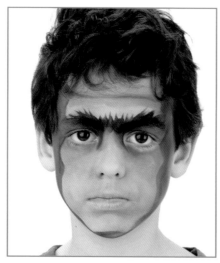

You will need:
Most people imagine Frankenstein's monster is going a bit moldy which is why he is painted green; you will need black, red, and purple as well.

3 The shape around the forehead is important if you want to make this monster look like Frankenstein. By shading the sides, you can make the forehead appear higher which gives Frankenstein his characteristic shape.

4 Using a fine paintbrush, make some thin black lines around the monster's face and then paint small lines across to create the stitching that holds him together. Add some red paint at the ends of the lines to look like blood if you want to be really gory.

1 Sponge a green base all over your model's face. This time it does not matter if the base is patchy as Frankenstein is a very shabby monster. Add some purple paint to your sponge and blend it into the cheeks and forehead to make unhealthy-looking shadows.

2 Using a wide brush and black paint, make a line across the eyebrows and nose. Extend it up the sides of the forehead. Take a sponge and pull the black paint down into the eye sockets and away from the side of the forehead. Soften the line across the nose by dragging the black paint toward the eyes.

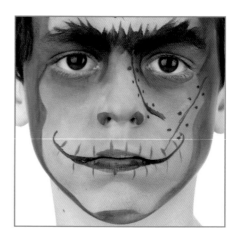

5 Paint Frankenstein's mouth with a thin purple line. Make sure he is smiling while you do this.

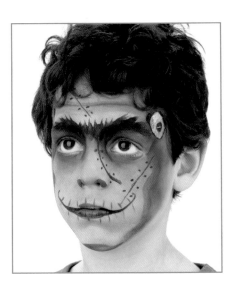

6 Finally paint a bolt on either side of Frankenstein's forehead. Use a medium straight-edged paintbrush, if you have one, to make a six-sided shape (like a square with a triangle on the top and bottom). Paint a little rod sticking into the head. Do the same on the other side of your model's forehead. Make sure the bolts are opposite one another.

Weird Werewolf

Is there anything more terrifying than finding out that you are a monster? Every month as the moon waxes, the moment comes closer and your palms begin to itch until the wolf hair breaks through and you are transformed. If this isn't the case and you really do want to be a monster, follow these simple steps.

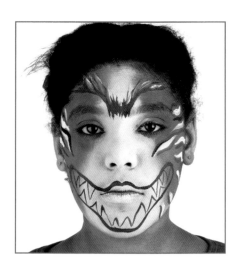

You will need:

The three most useful colors: black, white, and red make-up.

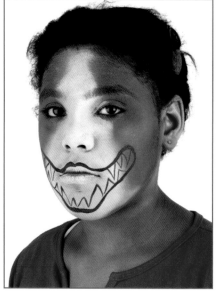

2 With black on your paintbrush, paint the outline of the werewolf's mouth. Make it curl up at the sides and extend down onto the chin. Fill it full of lots of sharp teeth.

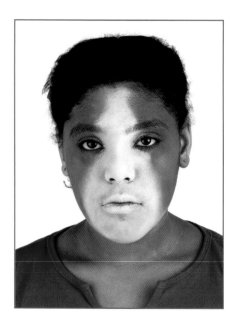

1 Sponge white over the model's eyes and down the center of the model's face. Mix black and white together to make gray. Sponge the rest of the face gray.

3 Paint wild shaggy eyebrows that come together in the center. Paint fur around the edge of the face using black, white, and gray. Try to make your marks end in a point by lifting the brush away from the face at the end of the brush stroke.

4 Ask your model to keep their eyes closed and outline an eye shape on the eyelid with black paint. It is important to let the make-up dry while the eyes are closed. Fill in the shape with white paint.

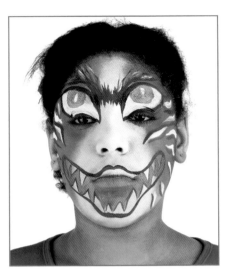

5 Take a clean brush and paint red eyes on the model's eyelids and paint red around the teeth inside the werewolf's mouth.

6 Finish by painting a black nose, snarl lines, and whiskers. Paint a black center to the red eyes. Paint the teeth white and outline them in black to make them show up.

Arty Tip:

You can make thick and thin marks with the same brush by pressing and lifting. The more pressure you use, the thicker the line will be. Always make sure the hairs on your brush are lying smoothly.

Wicked Witch

Witches are magic, so they can look any way they want to, although there is always something about them that gives the game away. The witch on this page is shown in her true colors, so if you want to look like her, you will need lots of make-up.

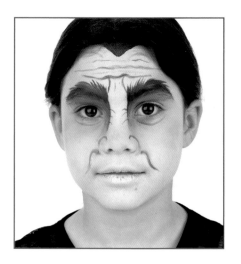

3 Ask your model to screw up her face and, with a fine brush, paint purple into all the lines that she can make on her face. You will be surprised how old she will look.

4 Paint a little spider's web in the outer corner of each eye as if it is coming from your model's smile lines and eyelashes.

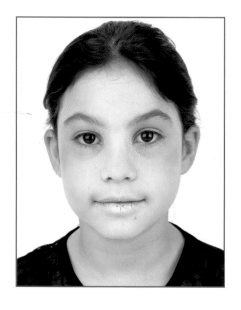

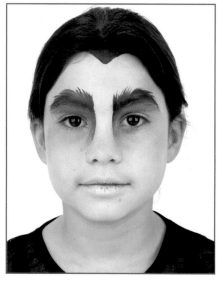

1 Start by sponging a very pale green base all over the model's face, then, without changing the sponge, dip it into some mauve paint. Sponge this into the eye sockets and at the sides of the forehead and cheeks. Use both colors on the sponge to soften and blend the colors together. You should try to make the base very even using only a thin layer of paint.

2 Use paint that matches the color of your model's hair to form a pointed hairline in the center of her forehead. Use dark purple paint for the model's eyebrows and soften the lower edge so that the eyebrows fade into the eye sockets. You can do this either with a sponge or with a large paintbrush.

You will need:
White, green, purple, red, and black paints.

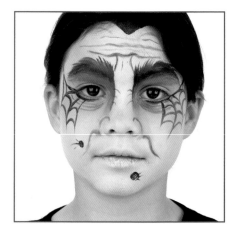

5 Paint red lines under her eyes. Add some warts and nasty moles using green or black paint.

6 Finish with a little lipstick and blusher, and even glitter – after all, even a wicked witch likes to look her best!

Magical Wizard

To be a wizard is everyone's ambition at the moment, but would you be a good wizard or an evil one? Whatever you decide, it is important to have a truly magical look. Wizards traditionally wear patterns of stars and moons on their cloaks and pointed hats. Just like their witch sisters, they can cast a very powerful spell so the make-up just has to be fantastic.

You will need:
White, blue, yellow, orange, gold, and silver face paints. If you have some pearlized colors, you could use them on this face painting but it is not essential.

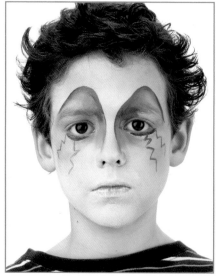

1 Start by sponging white paint all over the model's face, then blend blue into the eye sockets and on the forehead. Blend yellow onto the nose and cheeks. Blend blue into the sides of the face and around the chin. Use the orange on the yellow sponge to highlight the cheeks and parts of the forehead. Try to keep the colors delicate.

2 Mix up some darker blue paint and, with a medium brush, paint fine arching eyebrows. Start the eyebrow line below the natural brows on the side of the nose. Sweep the line up and above the real eyebrows before finishing back on the natural brow.

3 Paint a line under the eyes and create some zigzag lines at the corners of the eyes. Use gold and silver paint as well as blue.

Arty Tip:
You can paint a white drooping mustache and beard if you want your model to be an old wizard.

4 Paint a wizard logo on your model's forehead. If you are not sure how to paint this, you can trace the examples below and cut them out to make a stencil. You can buy special stencil paper or use an old unwanted photograph. Leave a border big enough to hold and sponge on to. Cut out all the black parts. Place the stencil on your model's head and, with a sponge, press the color onto the stencil. Be careful not to have the sponge too wet or the paint may run.

5 Paint stars on the wizard's cheeks. Add glitter to make him even more magical.

You Must Be Joking!

What is the difference between a drink of tea and a wizard?
One is a cuppa and the other is a sorcerer.

Vlad the Vampire

The vampire is a sinister creature that only comes to life at night. It spends the daylight hours sleeping in its coffin but at night it can flit like a bat, searching for innocent victims who have forgotten to hang garlic around their necks. Vampires love biting necks but they hate garlic. Unfortunately they hate mirrors too, so if you are made-up like a vampire, you may not be able to see yourself in the mirror!

You will need:

Black, white, and red paint. See how many other faces just use these three colors.

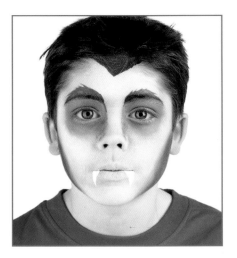

4 Use a clean brush to paint white fangs at the corner of the vampire's mouth.

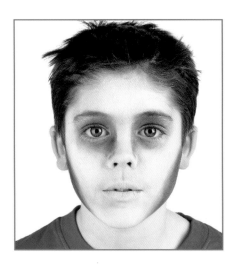

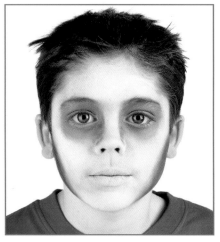

1 Start by sponging a white base all over the face, then, with a little black on the sponge, carefully create some shadows by lightly sponging the eye sockets, the sides of the nose, and the cheeks. You can make these shadows more definite by painting a line and then pulling the paint away from it with a sponge, but it looks more natural if you can do them freehand.

2 Sponge a little red below the eye and onto the cheeks.

3 Paint a black triangle with the point downward in the center of the hairline, and sponge black paint into the hair around the face. Don't worry, face paint washes out easily. Now paint in dark eyebrows.

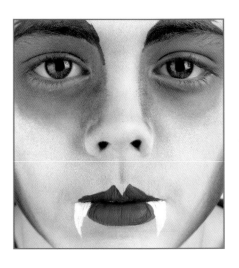

5 Mix up a dark red – with a little black in it – and use this to paint pointy lips.

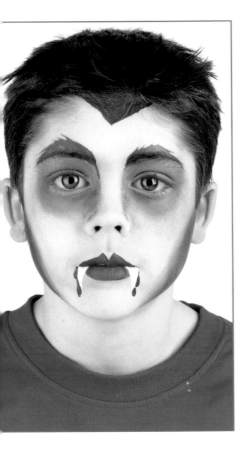

6 You can add some drops of red paint to represent blood dripping off the teeth.

Remember to take a photograph of your vampire – just in case they can't look at their own reflection in a mirror!

Fangtastic Fact!

The classic vampire tale *Dracula* was written in 1897 by Bram Stoker. He would have been delighted to know that Count Dracula has appeared in a great number of movies since he was first created.

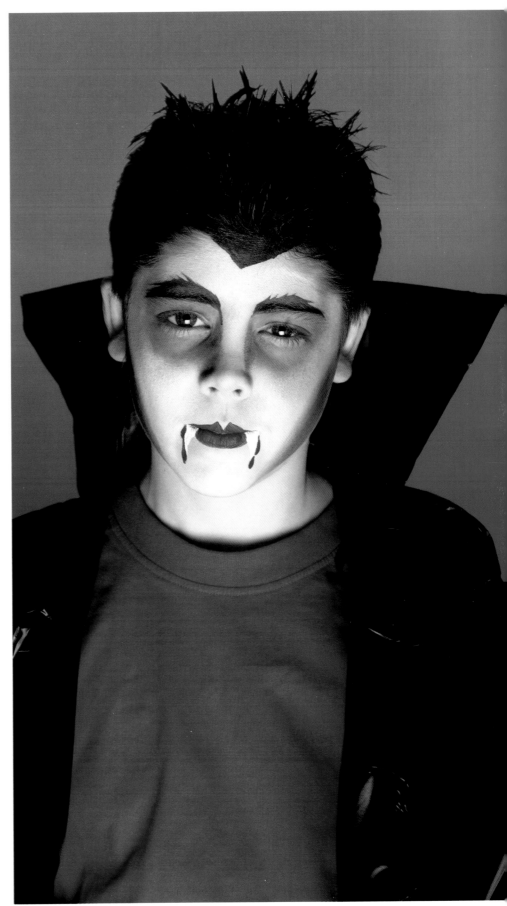

Ghoulish Ghost

Most people have never seen a ghost so it can be a bit tricky painting one. In movies, ghosts often look like monsters or sometimes like very frail old ladies. People who have seen ghosts often claim that they felt a cold shuddery feeling, or that objects moved about of their own accord. Perhaps a very realistic ghost would not be noticed at all. One thing is certain – however much like a ghost you look, you are only wearing face paint, so don't try walking through walls!

You will need:
Plenty of white paint and some red, purple, and black. A large piece of white material.

3 Rub the sponge into some red paint and make the color around the eyes a deeper reddish-purple. Paint dark lines under your model's eyes.

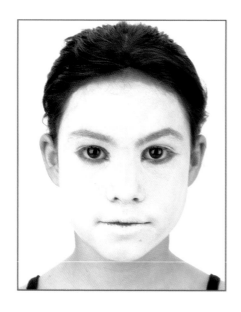

1 Ghosts may come in many shapes and forms, but a typical spook is very pale, so take a sponge with plenty of white paint on it and sponge a smooth base all over the model's face.

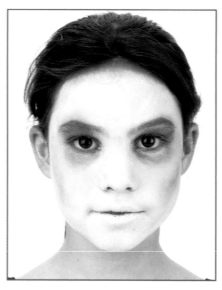

2 Rub your white sponge into some purple paint and gently blend purple around the eye sockets and under the cheekbones.

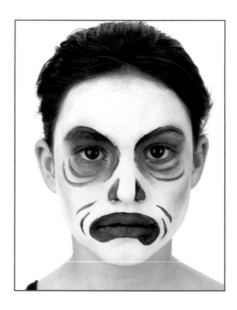

4 Use a large paintbrush to paint a sad wailing mouth. Use black paint or purple and red mixed together. Finish the disguise by draping a sheet or some spare white material over your model's head.

Arty Tip:

Because white is such a pale color it shows up streaks and patches in the base more than any other paint. Practice achieving a good white base and it will help you to become an excellent face painter. Be sure to have the sponge only slightly damp. Press the sponge onto the face rather than wiping it. Make sure you cover all the nooks and crannies of your model's face. If you ask your model to look up, you will be able to sponge right up to their eyes.

Haunting Humor

What did the old ghost say to the young ghost?
Only spook when you are spooken to.

Curse of the Mummy

The curse of the Egyptian mummy is a favorite movie subject. The mummy always appears as a gigantic bandaged corpse coming back to life with a hatred of everyone, especially archeologists and tomb raiders.

Real Egyptian mummies can be seen in museums and they are much smaller than the beautiful painted sarcophagus or case in which the mummy is preserved.

You will need:
A strong stomach for this gory face, some bandages and white, red, and black paint.

Safety Tip:
If you use crêpe bandages to dress up your model, be careful not to stretch them or they will feel too tight and be uncomfortable.

This make-up is for a frightening monster mummy with unwinding bandages and a disintegrating face.

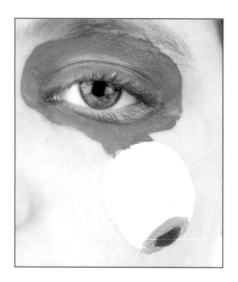

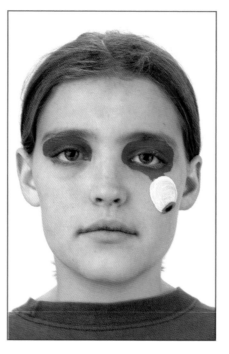

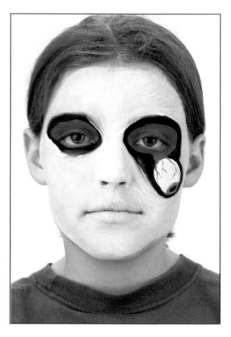

1 Start by painting a white eyeball under your model's left eye. Paint both the eyelids red, and apply red under the left eye as well. Paint a thick red line from below the eye to the painted eyeball.

2 Use black paint and a medium brush to outline all the painting so far. Take a damp sponge and pull the black paint away to create a shadow. Use a fine brush to paint red veins over the eyeball.

3 Next, using plenty of white paint, take your widest brush and paint bandages all around the face and over the mouth. Criss cross the bandages and sponge the lines to make them wider if your brush is not wide enough. Paint a piece of loose bandage dangling down near the eyeball.

Arty Tip:

It may seem quite difficult to paint a realistic eyeball but the good thing about horror faces is they look great even when the painting is simplified, so don't be scared to have a go.

Warning:

Never tie anything tightly around your model's neck.

4 Use a fine brush and black paint to outline the bandages. Paint a black oval on the red eyelid and on the eyeball.

Now you can ask your model to close their eyes for a photograph of the completed design before going out to terrorize everyone.

Spooky Skull

Skulls are not black and white although that is how lots of children's books show them. Skulls are a yellowy color – in fact the older the bones, the more yellowy and even brown they appear. So if you want to really frighten everyone, this realistic skull make-up should do the trick.

You will need:

White, yellow, green, and black paint.

One of the things that is easy about painting a skull is that your own head is exactly the right shape! By using black you can make shadows to hide all your nice healthy chubby bits, so that only your true bone structure will show. Are you sure you want to go on?

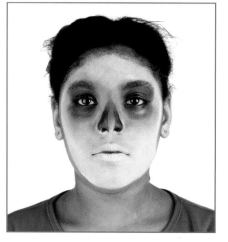

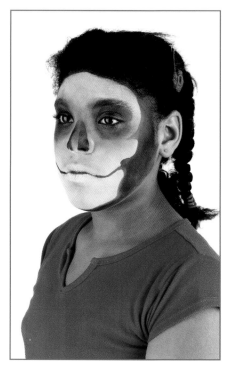

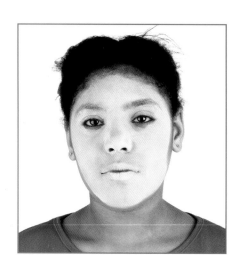

1 Start by sponging white and yellow together over the whole face. Add a little more yellow and a tiny bit of green to your sponge and work it into the color at the top of the forehead.

2 Use a clean sponge dipped in black to sponge over the eyelids and into the eye sockets. Change back to the pale colored sponge and soften the edge so that the center of the eye is very dark but the edge fades away. Use the same technique to color the nose black.

3 Use a large paintbrush dipped in plenty of black paint to outline the shadows around the skull. Use the brush to accentuate your model's cheekbone and paint in under it, in a step down to the jaw line.

4 Use a sponge to drag the paint away into the outside line of the face. This should make a strong shadow effect. With a fine brush, paint a line across the mouth and sharply up and out to the shadow line. Spread this line out where it meets the shadow to "cut off" the jawbone.

Dead Funny!

Why wouldn't the skeleton go to the party?
Because he had no body to go with.

5 Use the same brush to outline both rows of teeth. Look at your own teeth in the mirror to see how they are shaped and how they might appear on your model. Maybe some teeth could be missing!

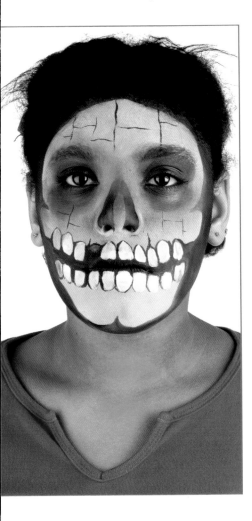

6 Finish the skull by painting in yellowy-white teeth and fine cracks in the bones.

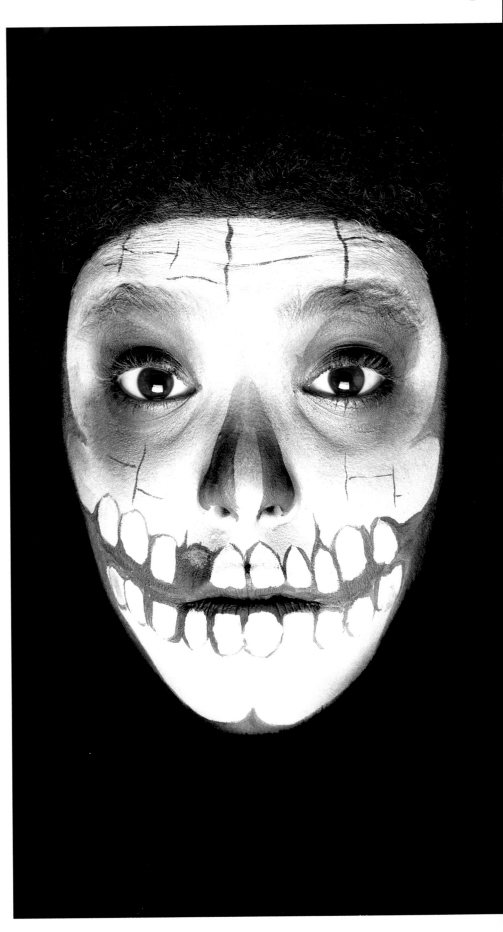

Fishy Faces

You will need:
Blue, green, and white make-up.
You can also use powder blusher
and gold crème make-up.

Neptune is the Roman god of the sea. Part fish, part man, he rules beneath the waves. He is always pictured with a sharp trident, rather like a Roman gladiator. The make-up for Neptune can easily be adapted for a mermaid. By looking at the similarities in these two fishy creations, you will learn how to adapt any make-up to your own design.

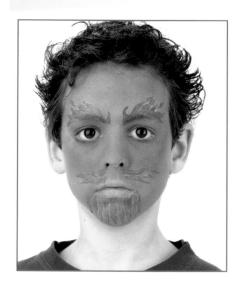

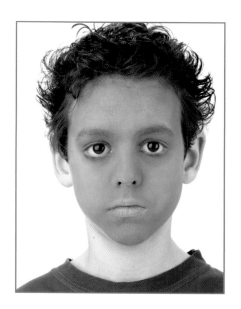

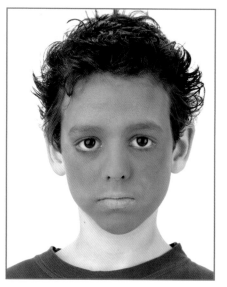

1 To paint the faces the way they look on this page, start by sponging a pale turquoise base. Use blues and greens with white blended together so that the end result is not just one flat color. Give Neptune some darker blues in his eye sockets.

2 For Neptune use an orange blusher, but for the mermaid try a pinker shade. If you have powder blusher, you could use them on this make-up but, if not, blend the colors in with a sponge.

3 Paint dark green curly eyebrows and a curling mustache and beard on Neptune. Use the point of the brush when you are painting curling lines.

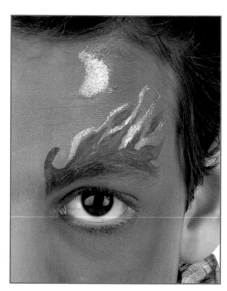

4 Finish with gold and silver lines to accentuate the dark colors. Paint a small pair of gold horns on Neptune, but not for the mermaid.

Arty Tip:

You can alter the shape of a face by shading the sides of the face, the chin, and the temples. It is surprising what a difference make-up can make to your model's appearance.

5 You can buy gold crème make-up for use on lips. It will look brighter than water-based gold paint, but don't use it all over the face as it does not wash off with soap and water (you need to use make-up remover). Use a special lip brush for crème make-up or it will spoil your other painting brushes. Always apply it last.

Mermaid

The instructions are for Neptune, but you can easily adapt them to create a shimmering mermaid, as you can see by looking at the picture below. Your mermaid should not look as fierce as Neptune, so give her smooth eyebrows, a wavy fringe, and long wavy eyelashes.

Arty Tip:

You might decide to paint scales onto Neptune. Look at the Space Monster on pages 58/59 to see how to paint them, or maybe the Wicked Witch on pages 28/29 would appeal more to your taste if she had eyelashes like the mermaid. You can just paint them on. If you want to be creative, you can mix and match the faces in this book.

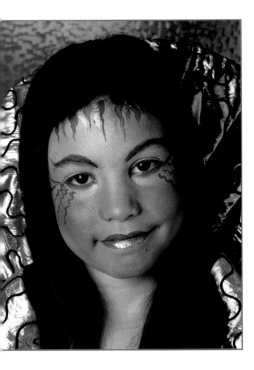

Leaping Dolphins

Everyone loves dolphins; they are very intelligent, agile creatures who seem to understand us even though their lives swimming in the ocean are so different from our own – except for those beach holidays when we can play and splash in the water a bit like them.

1 To paint dolphins leaping across a face, it is important to make a beautifully shaded base.

2 Use blue paint with any other colors that will suit your model. For example, blend blue and green or blue and pink in bands across the face. Make sure that the colors fade into each other with no hard edges, but possibly creating a new shade where they overlap.

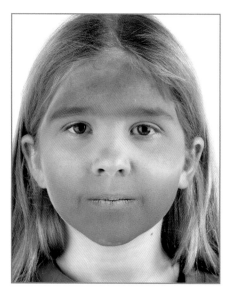

3 Use pearly white or gold on the forehead as well, if you have them, to give the face a shimmering look – like the sea with the sun shining on it.

4 Copy the dolphin shapes on this page, or trace them and cut out a stencil if you find dolphins difficult to paint freehand.

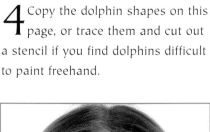

5 Take a little time to work out where to position the dolphins. It does depend on the size you want to paint them. The bigger the better, but it is advisable to start small until you have developed the knack of painting them. Try to make your dolphins dive and leap like real ones.

Arty Tip:
You could adapt this face to any sort of sea life, or even boats and seascapes. It is just a matter of practicing different silhouettes.

Arty Tip:
A perfectly blended base is the secret of success for every good face painter. Most designs look more interesting if you combine two or more colors into the base.

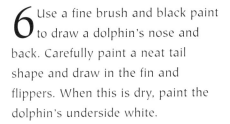

6 Use a fine brush and black paint to draw a dolphin's nose and back. Carefully paint a neat tail shape and draw in the fin and flippers. When this is dry, paint the dolphin's underside white.

7 You can paint water splashes and bubbles in white, and even add seaweed if you want to make your dolphin design more detailed. Use gold crème on your model's lips for a glistening effect, or you can leave them unpainted if you prefer a natural look.

Cutthroat Pirate

Pirates were nothing more than ocean-going robbers, creeping up on ships, breaking into them, and stealing all the wealth that the merchants and traders had managed to gather as they sailed around the world. The skull and crossbones flag was a terrible warning to honest sailors, but also to the pirates themselves if they were captured, because no mercy was shown to those wicked men and women.

You will need:

You will need to buy some special make-up called special effects wax to create the scars on this battered pirate. You can buy very good water-based wax, which washes off and is easy to use. Professional special effects wax can be taken off with make-up remover.

Of course many pirates bore terrible injuries from so much fighting. A pirate ship did not have a proper doctor, so pirates often carried lots of scars.

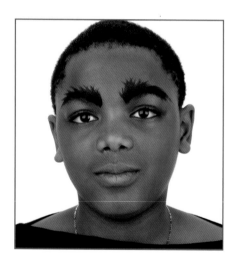

1 First of all rub a little reddish-brown into your model's skin to suggest a weather-beaten skin color. Then paint in big, bushy eyebrows.

2 To paint a black eye make the eyelid a greeny-yellow color. Paint blue and black underneath the eye. Blend these colors into the skin tone to look like a nasty bruise.

3 Use a teaspoon to take out a piece of special effects wax about 3/4in (2cm) long. Warm it in your hand by rolling it until it is soft and sausage-shaped. Be careful not to let it get too sticky. Gently press it onto your model's skin where you want to make a scar. Smooth out the edges and sponge the same reddish-brown skin color over the wax.

4 Make the center of the wax a bit redder as if it was sore. Use the edge of a piece of cardboard to form a line through the wax. It is important not to use anything sharp, as you cannot tell where your model's skin lies under the wax.

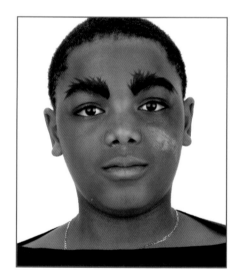

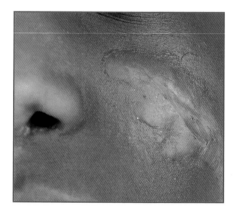

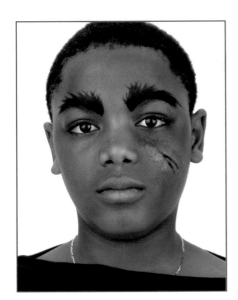

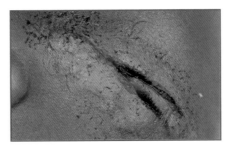

It is quite possible that your model will be feeling ill by now if they can see the wound in a mirror. If not, try doing one on their arm!

5 Paint a very thin black line into the middle of the cut to look like dried blood. Paint a dark red blood color into and around the edge of the cut. Sponge some blue around the scar to look like a bruise. Give your pirate a mustache or beard using black paint.

Shark Attack

The great white shark is known as an eating machine. It will attack and eat anything that is swimming about looking like lunch. Seals are the great white's favorite food but, unfortunately, surfers look very like seals as they paddle about on their surfboards. Great white sharks are very fast swimmers and can thrust their jaws out of the water to attack their prey.

You will need:

A variety of colors for the sunset background, but the shark is painted in black, white, and red.

This design for a shark rearing out of the water depends on getting the shark shape right. It must not be too wide or it will not look convincing.

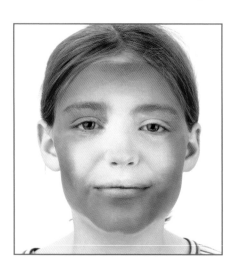

1 First blend a sunset sky across the top of your model's face. Use yellow, red, and pink blended seamlessly together. Blend blue around the sides of the face and chin. Leave the center of the face unpainted.

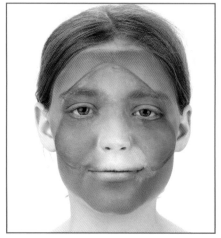

2 Use a broad brush and dark gray paint to draw the outline of the shark. It should start about level with your model's mouth and reach up to the forehead.

3 Use a clean sponge to drag the color into the middle of the face. It should get paler as you move away from the edge. If necessary add a little white to your sponge to help achieve this.

4 Paint a row of sharp, white zigzag teeth in an arch from one side of the face, over the nose, and down to the other side. Paint another arched row of teeth across the model's top lip.

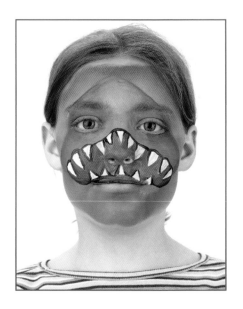

5 Paint the space around the zigzag teeth red – this is the inside of the shark's mouth.

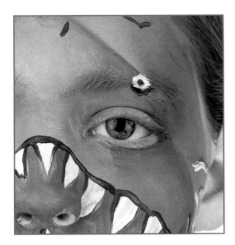

6 Paint black and white curved lines for gills on either side of the shark's mouth and paint eyes on the side of the shark's head above your model's own eyes. Outline the sharp teeth with a thin brush using black paint.

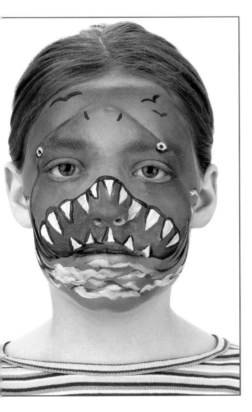

7 Paint white and blue swirls of water around the shark. You can even paint in some scavenging seagulls as silhouettes against the evening sky.

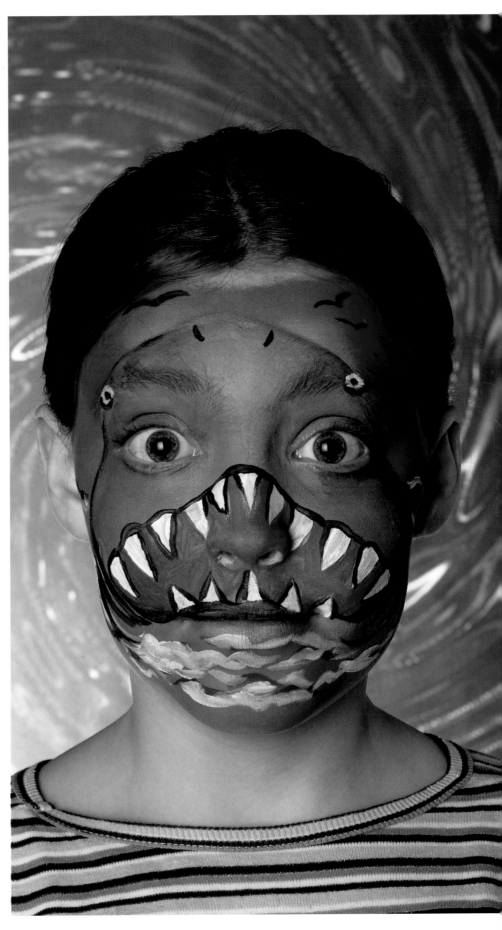

King of the Jungle

This make-up is so popular, it is usually the first design that face painters want to try. It remains a firm favorite because however fierce lions are, we all love them. They look so proud – no wonder the lion has earned the title of king of the jungle.

All members of the cat family make great designs for face painting. See if you can adapt this lion make-up by painting on markings to make a tiger or a leopard to add to your list of scary animal faces.

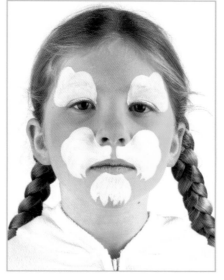

1 Sponge yellow paint all over your model's face, blend red into the cheeks and down the nose to make an orange color.

You will need:
Yellow, red, white, and black face paint.

2 Use a wide brush to paint white cloud shapes above the eyes and over the eyebrows. Paint more cloud shapes across the top lip, up onto the cheeks and around the mouth. Paint a white beard under the mouth.

3 Paint a little black nose across the end of your model's nose; paint a line down from the middle of the nose to the lips. Paint the top lip black. Extend it outward a little way and curve it upward into a smile.

4 Paint the model's bottom lip using deep pink paint mixed by using red and white together.

5 Take a clean, fine brush and outline the white areas around the eyes with black paint. Continue the lines down each side of the nose. Next paint a line under each eye, give them a little curl at the end. Outline the white muzzle around the mouth and the pink tongue.

6 Paint some dots on either side of the top lip and add some fine lines for whiskers. Use the tip of the pointed brush; it is easiest if you keep the brush at right angles to the face as you do this.

Jungle Fashion

Only male lions have long hairy manes, the female lions have short hair. Pick a style to suit your model.

7 Mix up a darker orange and, with a clean brush, paint in curling lines across the forehead and down the sides of the face to represent a lion's mane.

8 Or you can just let your model's hair down if it is long enough, and brush it so that it looks like a wild mane.

Graceful Giraffe

Did you know that although a giraffe has such a long neck, it only has the same number of bones in it as yours does? Giraffes are so tall that their knees are level with a person's chest. When they want to reach the ground to eat, they have to spread their legs apart, but most of the time they eat leaves from tall trees.

Giraffes have strange irregular markings, a bit like a jigsaw, all over them. This makes them very interesting to turn into a design for face painting.

You will need:
Brown, white, red, and black face paint.

Arty Tip:
The illusion of a long nose does not work if your model smiles but it looks quite realistic when the mouth is closed.

1 Giraffes have little horns on top of their heads. If your model has long hair, make little bumpy horns with a hairband – see pages 10/11.

2 Blend a creamy fawn color all over your model's face and a slightly darker brown down the center of the face. Add just a little red to this at the temples.

3 Using a wide brush and dark gray paint, draw a line either side of the forehead down through the inner corner of the eye, and either side of the nose, until just level with the nostrils. Flare the line out and curve it round to the top lip. Use a sponge to drag the paint into the center to make a soft gray-brown nose.

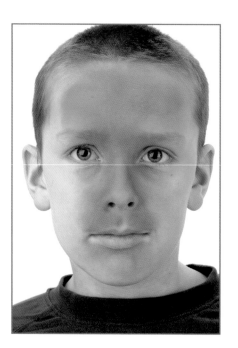

4 Paint the same gray-brown across the lower lip and under the mouth in a "U" shape.

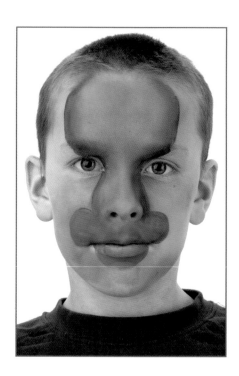

5 Use a wide brush and darker brown paint to make blocks of brown on the forehead and cheeks.

6 Paint black ears in a roughly triangular shape diagonally across the eyebrows. Use a soft gray-brown to color them in.

7 Paint a thin black line along each eyelid and under the eyes and extend little lines from them to look like eyelashes.

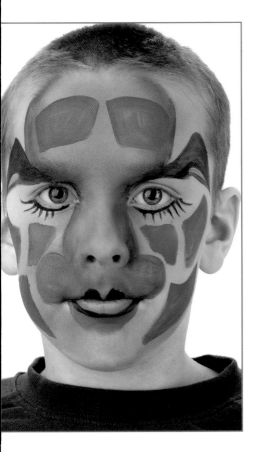

8 Paint marks on the top lip for nostrils and add a black line under the lower lip for a mouth.

Lazy Lizard

If you are feeling lazy and just want to bask in the sun, this is the perfect make-up for you. Lizards are cold-blooded creatures so they need to keep warm all the time. The warmer they are, the more active they can be.

You will need:

You will need two shades of green to paint this make-up. You can make a paler shade of green by mixing dark green with white and a little yellow. You will also need copper or brown and black paint.

1 Start by sponging pale green over the bottom lip and the lower part of your model's face. Extend the color up at the sides of the face, until level with the middle of the ears.

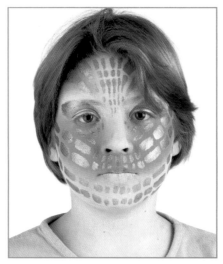

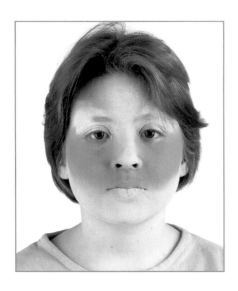

2 Sponge a little of the pale green down the center of your model's face. Take a clean sponge and paint dark green all over the rest of the face. Blend it into the center of the face but just allow the colors to meet, without blending, on the lower part of the face.

3 Paint a slanting copper or brown almond shape on each of your model's eyelids. Take a clean straight-cut brush and, again, using copper or brown paint, make a pattern of marks by simply laying the brush on its flat side, over your model's face. Make some large rectangular shapes and some smaller squares, and continue this all over the green base paint.

4 Paint black shapes on either side of the nostrils as shown in the following picture.

5 Use a medium-sized brush and black paint to draw a line from the middle of the ear out across the face and then curve it down and across the mouth. Continue up and out to the other ear. The line should be the same both sides and should meet the mouth at each corner.

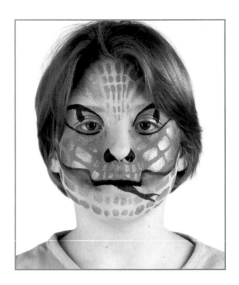

6 Paint black outlines around the almond shapes on your model's eyelids and draw a black line through the middle of the lid to form a pupil. Finally, paint a black forked tongue flicking out of the mouth.

Warning:
If you are allowed to color your model's hair, only use temporary colors which will wash out immediately after use. **Never use permanent hair color or dye.**

Ugly Warthog

This creature is not very handsome – even his name tells you how ugly he is! However, it is great fun to do really ugly make-ups. Although it is quite an unusual design, warthogs turn up regularly in cartoon movies, and you could almost say that they are now becoming popular. The tusks are so big you have to be careful how you place them. No doubt, real warthogs have to be careful with them too!

You will need:
Brown, pink, black, and white face paint.

3 Paint a pink triangular shape over the model's nose, spreading onto the cheeks. Outline it with black paint and soften the black edge with a sponge.

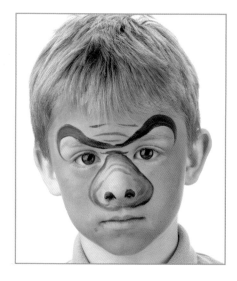

4 Paint a few thin black wrinkle lines on the nose and forehead.

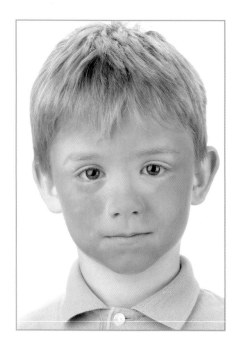

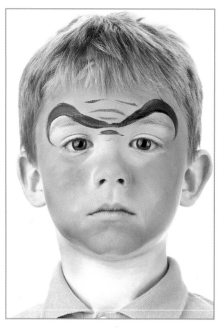

1 Sponge a mid-brown all over the model's face; make it paler over the eyes and blend a little pink into the cheeks and around the eyes. Paint a shaggy gray and yellowy-brown tuft of hair at the top of the forehead.

2 Paint black eyebrows sweeping out and round the eyes. Do not paint a line under the eyes, as you want to make them look small and piggy.

5 Use a medium-sized brush to paint the white tusks. Position them either side of the lower lip on the cheeks. Paint a gray line along the model's mouth and extend it to the tusks and a little way beyond them.

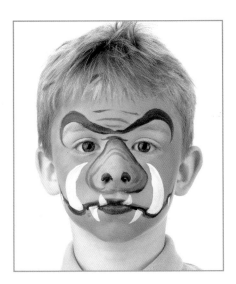

6 Paint a gray circle around the base of each tusk; fill it with a little pink. Add some more long white teeth. Paint the nostrils black and outline the tusks if they need to stand out more.

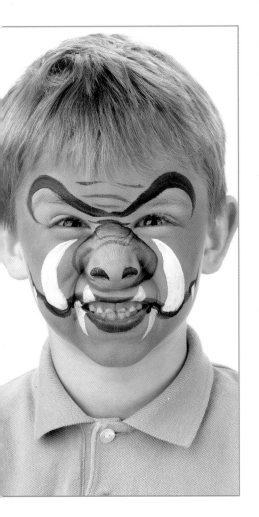

Little Green Alien

This is the original little green alien from outer space. However, your alien could be silver or even blue. The final design is up to you and you can paint an alien the way you feel an alien should look. As you develop your own style, you will find that you can paint faster. Face paint dries very quickly so you will probably find that fast painting gets better results.

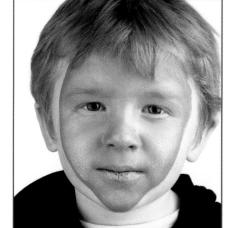

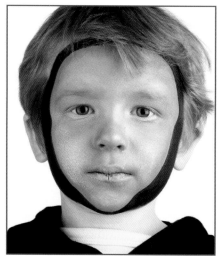

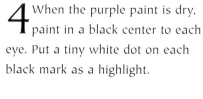

4 When the purple paint is dry, paint in a black center to each eye. Put a tiny white dot on each black mark as a highlight.

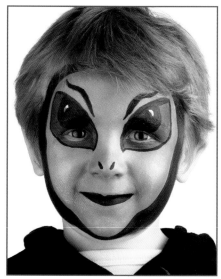

1 Start the alien by painting an outline in a metallic green. Make the shape wide at the top and very narrow at the chin – a bit like a balloon. Sponge the center green.

You will need:

Metallic face paint would look good – mix silver and gold with other colors to make a metallic finish.

2 Use a wide brush to paint a black outline all around the alien's head. Use a sponge to drag this color away into shadows at the sides of the face.

3 Paint big purple eyes on the model's eyelids and up onto the forehead. Outline them with black and paint a thin black eyebrow along the top edge of each alien eye.

5 Put two small black dots on the end of your model's nose to make the alien's nostrils. Paint your model's lips black. Do not paint outside the natural lip line.

Arty Tip:

Remember you can choose to add to this design. Perhaps your alien has sharp fangs or a forked tongue?

Space Monster

If you know someone who has seen a space monster, ask them to tell you what it looked like; if not, you can let your imagination run wild and paint the craziest monster in the universe.

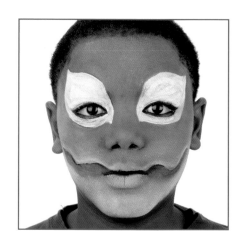

3 Paint a black wavy line across the model's face through the mouth. Use a sponge to soften the line and to make a shadow. Paint a white line above it and soften that to create a highlight.

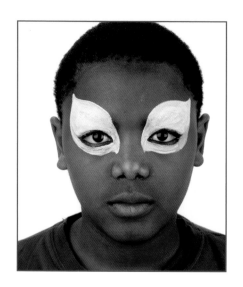

1 Start by painting huge white eyes on your model. Position them so that the inner corners touch the side of your model's nose and the outer corners reach up to the sides of the forehead.

Arty Tip:

To help you balance the brush on the face without pressing too hard (for example when you need to paint a fine line), place your little finger on your model's face while holding the paintbrush with your first finger and thumb. Remember to keep your little finger still so that it does not smudge the make-up.

2 Take a wide brush and outline the eyes with green paint. Use a sponge to drag the green away and then sponge green over the rest of the top half of the face. Blend yellow with the green on the lower part of the face and across the top lip.

You will need:

Green, yellow, black, white, and blue face paint and glitter.

4 Outline a big wide nose from the inner corner of the space monster's eyes to either side of your model's nose. Soften the edge with a sponge. Paint big black nostrils and shade the end of your model's nose to complete the illusion.

5 Use a fine brush and dark blue paint to draw big scales on the face. Be careful to use only the pointed tip of the brush to do this.

6 Ask your model to close their eyes and paint big golden-yellow eyes on the eyelids. When you paint the black center of each eye, leave a little white highlight which will make the eyes look even more realistic.

7 Finish the space monster by painting in plenty of sharp teeth and add glitter to the scales.

Mechanical Robot

There are so many different sorts of robots. We tend to think of them as human-shaped bits of metal and you can represent that quite easily if you want, but this robot is more mechanical. He has all sorts of gadgets and bits that whirr around.

1 Sponge a base color over the face leaving the eyes, nose, and mouth areas clear, as shown in the picture below. This design has a blue and mauve blend but you could choose colors to match your model's clothes.

2 Mix up some silver paint and, using a wide brush, paint a rectangular bar across your model's eyes and forehead. The lower line of the shape should run just beneath your model's eyes. The shape should be just wider than the real eyes.

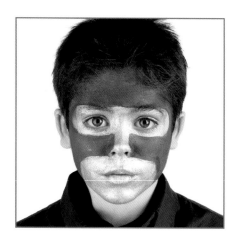

3 Paint a silver line down the center of your model's nose. Then paint a hexagonal shape from the nose to the chin. Fill in the shape with silver.

4 Use a fine brush and black paint to outline what you have done. Paint a thick black bolt at the bridge of the nose. Paint in the lines to define the sides of the hexagonal shape. Paint a semicircle on the top lip under the nose.

You will need:
Blue, mauve, silver, black, yellow, and red face paint.

5 Use a clean brush and bright yellow paint to create a semicircle at either end of the bar across the eyes. Outline the shape in black. When it is dry, paint in a fine zigzag filament with black paint.

6 Paint another light bulb onto one of your model's cheeks. Join it to the robot with black and white lines, like a screw fitting, and wild curly red wires. You will need the base to be completely dry to paint details like this over it.

7 On the other cheek, paint a "gadget" and another red curly wire. Make sure that the wires join onto the robot's body with a circle of black paint.

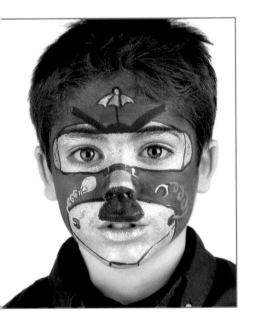

8 Paint black flaps sticking up from the top of the robot and paint a "whirly" shape, that looks a bit like an umbrella. If you prefer, you could paint a radar dish or an antenna.

Solar Storm

The solar system is made up of our Sun and all the planets. A solar storm occurs when there are violent eruptions on the surface of the Sun and huge flares of energy shoot out. Scientists can study solar storms when there is an eclipse because they can clearly see the hot gas erupting from the Sun, or the corona as it is called.

The make-up for a solar storm face is very dramatic and the style is rather different from the other faces in the book. It is more abstract and expressive. You can have great fun with this face, putting on lots of glitter and using all your colors.

3 Now the fun begins. Fill in your Sun with streaks of hot pinks, reds, orange, gold, yellow, and white.

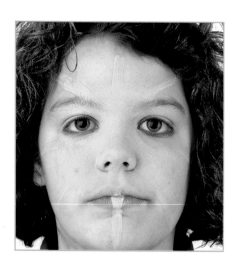

1 Start by sponging a pale yellow circle in the center of your model's face. Create a star shape by painting four lines right across the face.

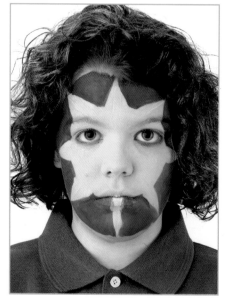

2 Next mix up dark blue and using a wide brush outline the star shape but leave a triangular space around each point. Use a sponge to blend the dark blue background together. You could put some purple on the sponge and also turquoise. The background color will look very rich and vibrant if you blend other colors with the blue.

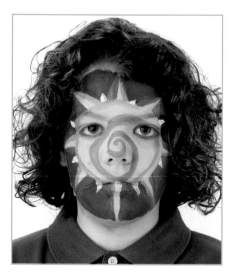

4 Paint a wild spiral of bright orange all around the middle of the Sun.

5 Use a fine brush and black paint. Make sure it is well mixed so that it makes a strong contrast. Paint crazy zigzag outlines around all the points of the Sun and add a contrasting spiral.

6 If you have gold crème, use it to complete this design; if not, finish by painting gold or yellow zigzags in the spaces between the points and adding plenty of glitter.

Useful Information

Cleaning Up:

When you have finished your face painting, you will need to know how to wash face paints off. Start by using plenty of water. Face paints are water-soluble so the wetter you make your face, the quicker the make-up will come off. Use a flannel and warm water with a little soap. Don't get soap in your eyes though. When you have finished washing, if you still look a bit painty use some cleansing cream or baby lotion on face wipes to remove any remaining paint. If you have a tendency to dry skin, the paint may stain your skin slightly and it would probably be better to use only warm water and cleansing cream rather than soap. Don't dry your face on a towel until all the paint has been removed and make sure you leave the sink clean! Wash your brushes carefully and use shampoo and conditioner to keep the bristles in top condition. You can put your sponges into the washing machine to get them really clean and soft. Always tidy up immediately after you have been painting, so that you can be sure that your paints are clean and ready for the next make-up session.

Useful Contacts

You can contact the Face Painting Association in the UK for advice and further information. Telephone: 07000 322372 (calls are charged at the national rate) or visit their website at www.facepaint.co.uk

There are plenty of sites on the Internet relating to face painting, but surf with care. A good site to start with is www.snazaroo.com/links.htm which lists a wide variety of face painting links from all over the world.